Math 'a' Maze

PUFFIN BOOKS

An imprint of Penguin Random House

PUFFIN BOOKS

USA | Canada | UK | Ireland | Australia
New Zealand | India | South Africa | China | Singapore

Puffin Books is part of the Penguin Random House group of companies
whose addresses can be found at global.penguinrandomhouse.com

Published by Penguin Random House India Pvt. Ltd
4th Floor, Capital Tower 1, MG Road,
Gurugram 122 002, Haryana, India

First published in Puffin Books by Penguin Random House India 2018

Text, design and illustrations copyright © Quadrum Solutions Pvt. Ltd 2018
Series copyright © Penguin Random House India 2018

ISBN 9780143444831

Design and layout by Quadrum Solutions Pvt. Ltd

Printed at Repro India Limited

www.penguin.co.in

Dear Moms and Dads,

In the twenty-first century, logic skills have become an intrinsic part of the skills required for children to grow into confident adults. To be ready to absorb more complex mathematical concepts later in life, maths readiness has assumed greater importance than ever before. That is why it has become ever so important to prep children while they are young and eager to learn.

The Fun with Maths series seeks to do just that—let children loose on the joy of applying logic and building mathematical skills as they go.

We created these books for children to explore the wonders of mathematics. Here's a peek into what they will learn (without even knowing they have learnt it):

1 Mathematical operations such as addition, subtraction, division and multiplication

2 Logical reasoning and spatial awareness

3 Patterns, symmetry and geometry

4 Application of mathematics in everyday life

It's been great creating this series with my highly charged Quadrum team: maths experts Krupa Shah and Madhavi Nathan, who spent hours crafting each page; Himani, who designed every page into a visual treat; Dinesh, who provided creative guidance; Kushal, who painstakingly laid out every number and sign; Bishnupriya and Ruby, who read and re-read every word; and Kunjli, who was the conscience of the entire series. And, of course, the Puffin team, Sohini and Mriga, who added value at every step. When you have a great team, you're bound to have a great book.

Thank you, guys!

Sonia Mehta

PS: We'd love your feedback, so do write in to us at

funlearningbooks@quadrumltd.com

Hello Kids

I'm sure you love solving mazes. It's great fun to get lost in a maze, and then find your way out of it.

Get set for some a-mazing math fun

Here are a whole load of amazing mazes for you to solve—but with a twist. It's not enough to just find your way out. You will have to solve some fun math puzzles as you go along, which will give you the cue to the right way out.

And guess what! While you're having fun solving the mazes, you're also going to get some great math practice. Math-a-Maze is a super fun way to sharpen your math skills. You will get to apply addition, subtraction, counting, sequencing and some other cool skills along the way, like spatial and logical skills. So here is what you need to do:

1. Gaze at the maze
2. Solve the sum
3. Find the pattern or the logic
4. Jump right in to find your way out!

Math-o-Bot Challenge

Watch out for the Math-o-Bot challenge board game maze. This is a game you can play again and again, with your friends, cousins and even your parents. You'll probably beat them all.

So are you ready to exercise those grey cells?

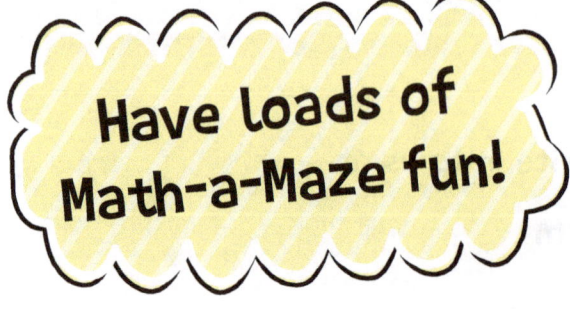

Have loads of Math-a-Maze fun!

Green Grass

Help the hungry cow reach the grass. Compare the numbers using the < and > signs. Think of the signs as arrows leading you through the maze.

 Moo!

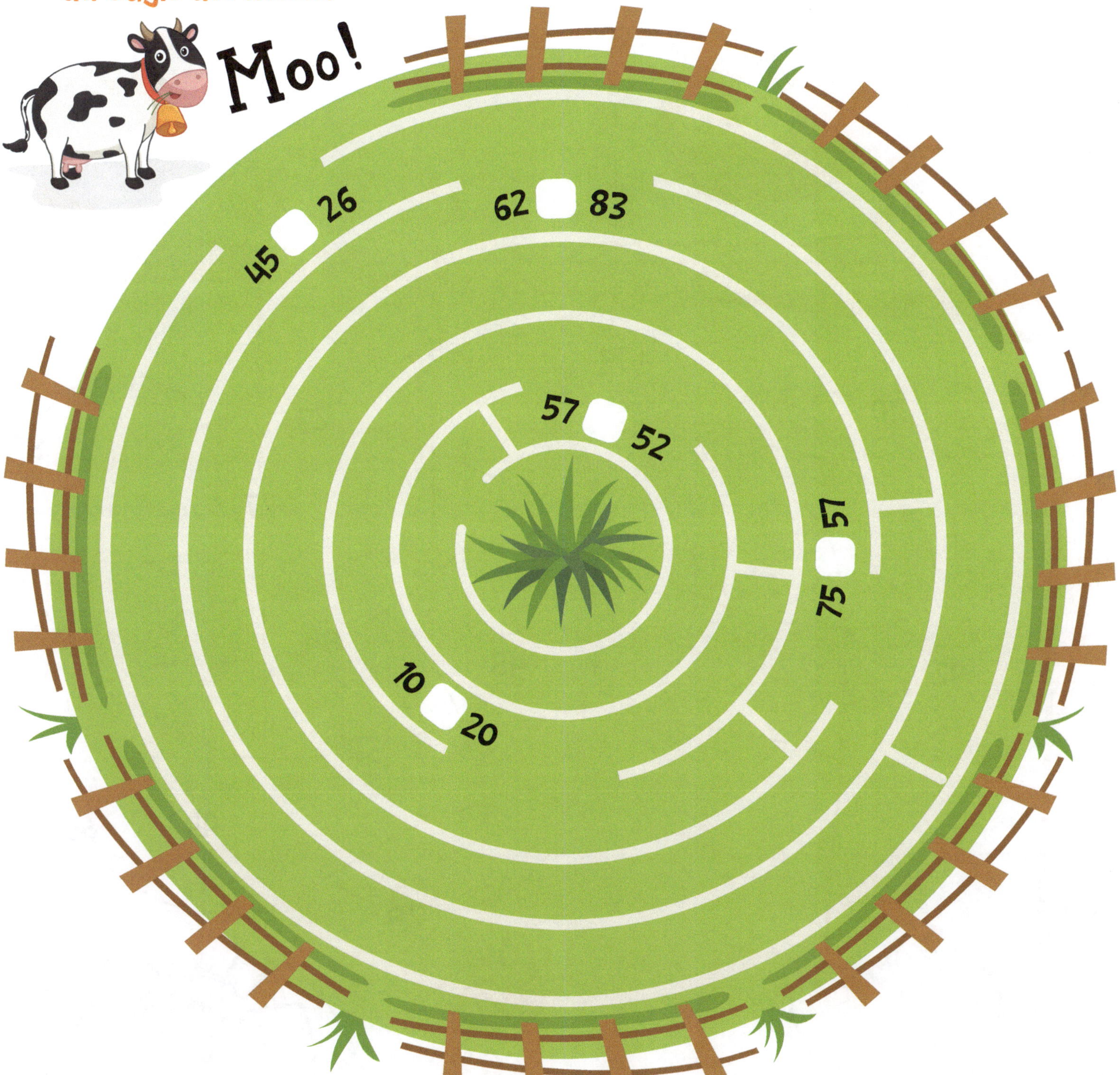

45 ☐ 26   62 ☐ 83

57 ☐ 52

75 ☐ 57

10 ☐ 20

Little Birdie

Help the little birdie get to the worm. Follow the numbers on each string. You get the worm if the numbers are in the ascending order.

Cheesy Bites

Help the mouse get to the cheese. Add the numbers in the maze. If the numbers add up to an even number, you are on the right path.

Even numbers have 0, 2, 4, 6, 8 in the units place.

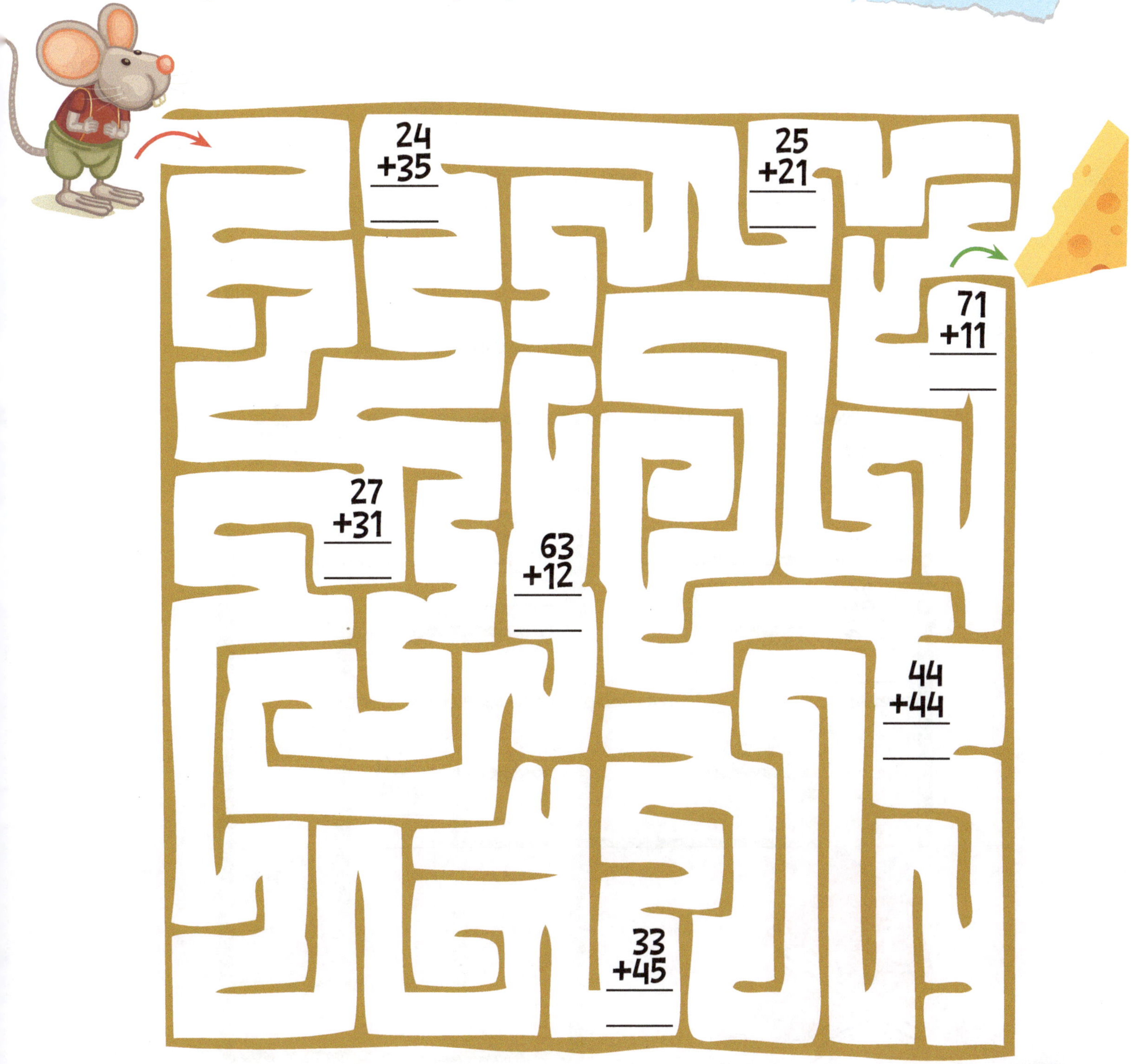

24
+35
____

25
+21
____

71
+11
____

27
+31
____

63
+12
____

44
+44
____

33
+45
____

Sneaky Laces

The laces need to reach the sneakers. Add the numbers in the maze. If the numbers add up to an odd number, you are on the right path.

Math-It

Odd numbers have 1, 3, 5, 7, 9 in the units place.

41
+ 4
———

32
+ 5
———

11
+11
———

13
+ 12
———

22
+ 6
———

24
+ 5
———

Snail Meal

This snail is hungry. Help it get to the cabbage. Add the numbers and highlight the answers where the sum is 78 to reach the snail's meal.

53
+33
___

34
+11
___

43
+35
___

26
+52
___

27
+51
___

Hundred Plus

In the mazes below, find a route through the garden to help the girl get to the flowers. Solve the addition sums, and if the answer is more than 100, you are on the right path.

Remember to carry forward when your number is bigger than 9.

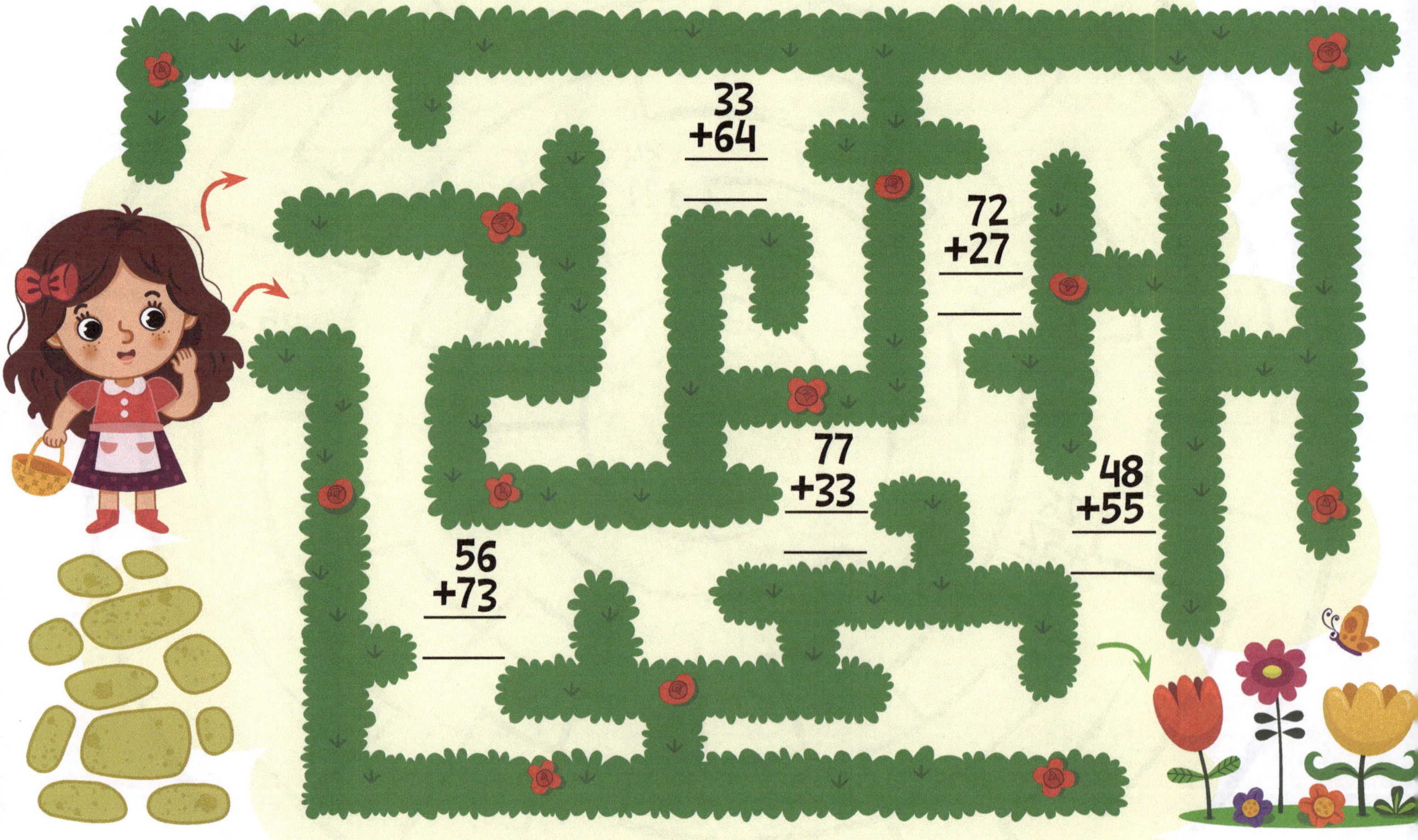

$$33 + 64$$

$$72 + 27$$

$$77 + 33$$

$$48 + 55$$

$$56 + 73$$

All Aboard!

Can you help the school bus driver take as many children to school on his route? He needs to pick up 32 children to ensure that his bus is full. Guide him along the maze from the depot to the school so that he has a full bus! Remember that whatever path you choose, going back the way you came is not allowed.

START

6

5

3

4

3

5

8

7

2

5

6

SCHOOL

FINISH

Secret Kingdom

Help the king reach his kingdom by following the odd–even rule. He must take a route wherein the numbers are odd–even–odd–even.

Math-It

You must try different ways to get to your answer.

5	2	55	14	21
14	13	26	31	24
7	18	27	6	16
12	9	38	15	1
3	8	11	6	5

Treasure Trail

There is a hidden treasure in your backyard. Can you find the treasure by subtracting the sums given below? Look for number 17 along the route to reach the treasure.

$$56 - 31$$

$$57 - 40$$

$$89 - 72$$

$$99 - 82$$

$$46 - 16$$

$$45 - 23$$

$$88 - 27$$

$$28 - 11$$

$$29 - 21$$

$$74 - 24$$

Lost Lion

Help Roar the lost lion reach his den. Solve the sums in the maze and mark the odd number answers to find your way.

$$\begin{array}{r} 57 \\ -23 \\ \hline \end{array}$$

$$\begin{array}{r} 65 \\ -31 \\ \hline \end{array}$$

$$\begin{array}{r} 86 \\ -44 \\ \hline \end{array}$$

$$\begin{array}{r} 87 \\ -34 \\ \hline \end{array}$$

$$\begin{array}{r} 88 \\ -43 \\ \hline \end{array}$$

Escape Plan

Can you help the worm escape so that the bird doesn't eat it? Start with number 50. Subtract the numbers in the way to find your path. You must be left with zero.

The first number always has to be bigger than the second number.

50

12

35

38

20

12

20

13

5

Best Friends

Help the dog meet his master. Solve the sums along the way; if the answers are less than 45, you are on the right path.

$$\begin{array}{r} 66 \\ -39 \\ \hline \end{array}$$

$$\begin{array}{r} 85 \\ -26 \\ \hline \end{array}$$

$$\begin{array}{r} 63 \\ -15 \\ \hline \end{array}$$

$$\begin{array}{r} 70 \\ -42 \\ \hline \end{array}$$

$$\begin{array}{r} 64 \\ -29 \\ \hline \end{array}$$

$$\begin{array}{r} 73 \\ -12 \\ \hline \end{array}$$

Flutter Flutter

Help the butterflies meet. Mark the numbers where the addition is correct to find your path.

Math-It

Repeated addition is adding the same number again.

4 + 4 + 4 + 4 = 12

2 + 2 + 2 + 2 = 10

5 + 5 + 5 = 15

3 + 3 + 3 = 9

2 + 2 = 4

7 + 7 + 7 = 37

High Five

In the maze below, find a way through the cactus. Mark the numbers that are multiples of 5 to help you.

51

12

40

20

57

46

15

60

Math-It

The correct numbers will always have 5 or 0 in the units place.

55

35

Building Bricks

Can you help the mason lay some bricks? Circle the numbers that are multiples of 2, 3 or 5 to find the way.

12

17

6

32

40

16

25

30

15

37

21

24

31

20

School Rounds

The principal has to visit every classroom before he leaves for the day. Which path should he follow? He must cross each classroom only once.

Math-It

Is there a room he can cross more than once?

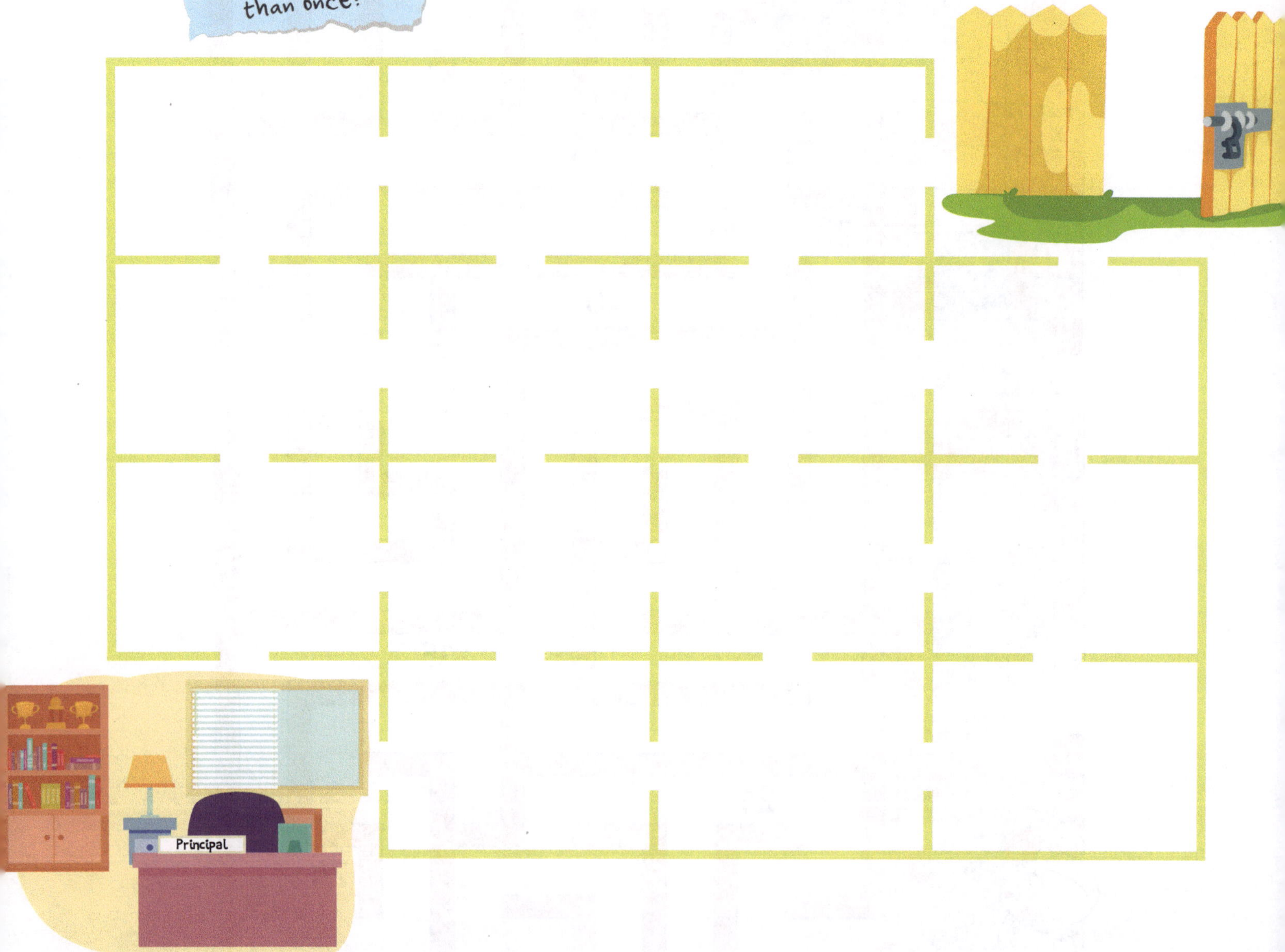

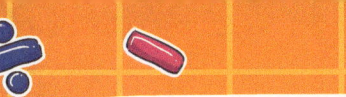

Clothes Line

Help Rita get to the clothes line to pull down the clothes before they get wet in the rain. Circle the number if equal grouping by 3 is possible as they will lead you to the terrace.

Equal grouping is also called division.

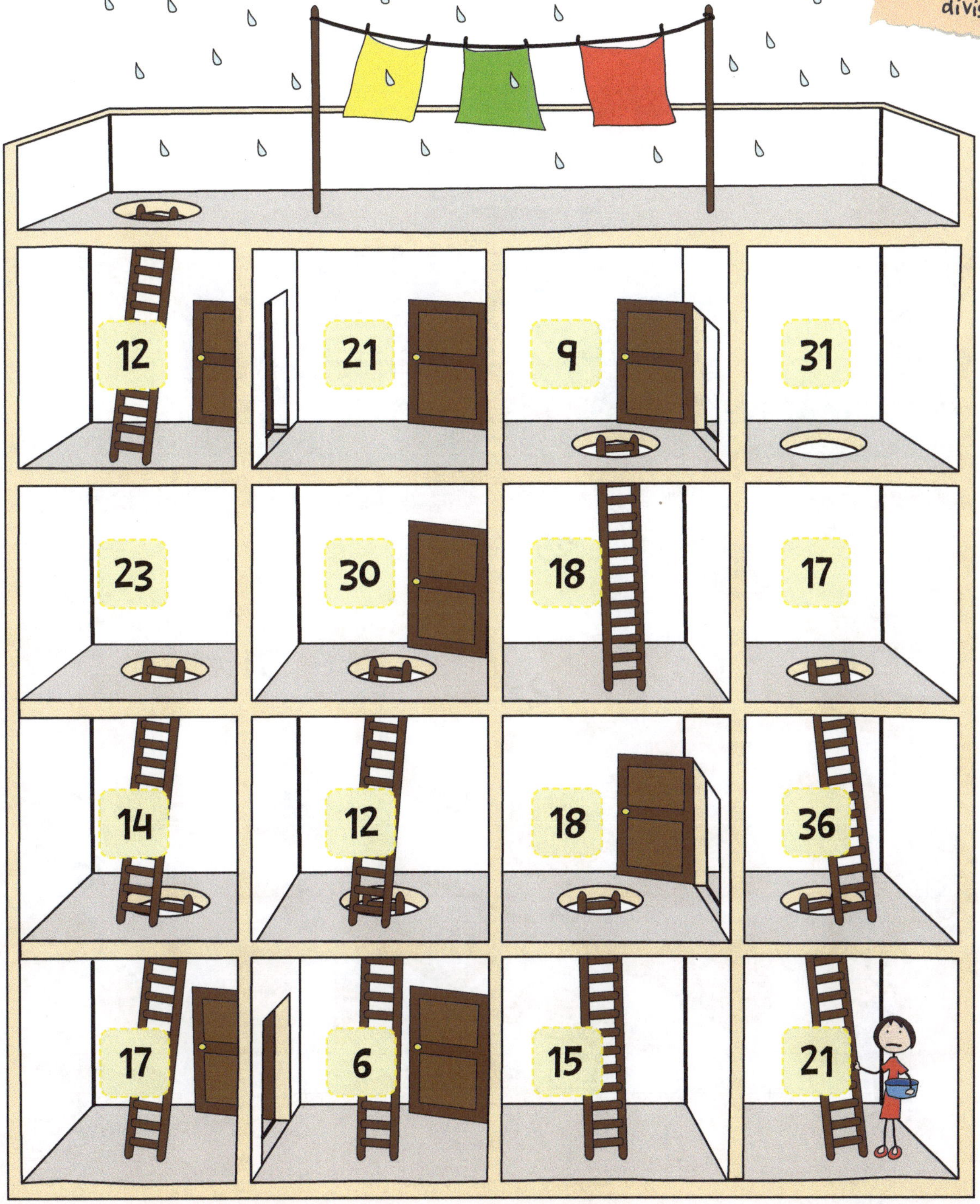

12	21	9	31
23	30	18	17
14	12	18	36
17	6	15	21

Treasure Hunt

Help Tim reach the treasure by digging his way through. Mark the numbers if they can be divided into equal groups (like 5 + 5 or 4 + 4) as they will lead you to the end.

Math-It

An even number can always be divided into two groups.

99 - 82

Peachy

Follow this pattern to help the worm get out of the maze.

Math-It

This is an A B C pattern.

Pathway

Follow the pattern **4**, **7**, **10**, **13** and so on to find a path out of the maze.

Add 3 to the previous number to get the pattern.

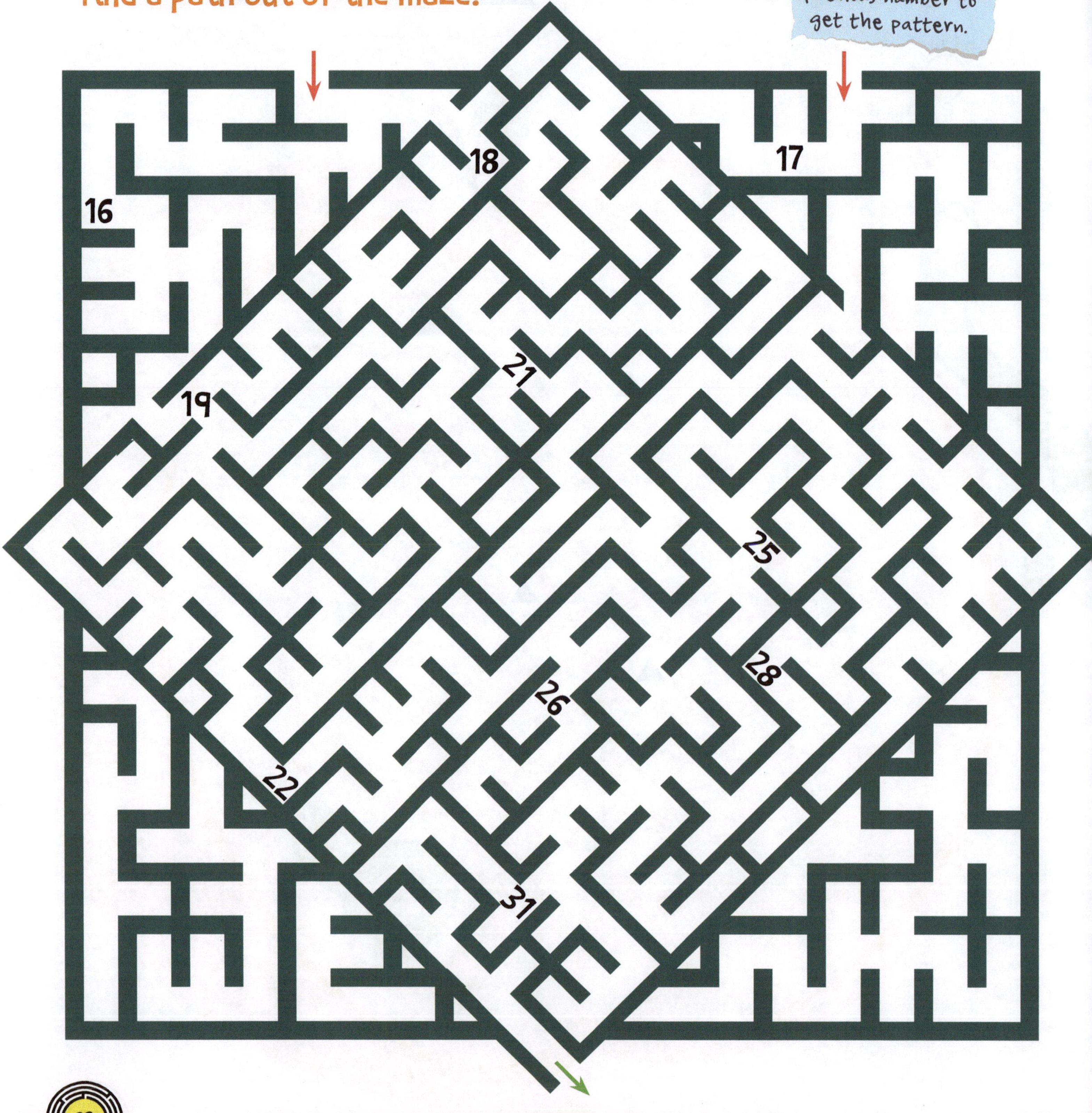

16

18

17

19

21

25

28

26

22

31

Piggy Piggy

Help the piglet reunite with his family saying 'clomp oink oink'. Identify and follow the pattern so that baby pig can be happy.

Math-It
The pattern follows the ABB rule.

oink · oink · clomp · oink · oink · clomp · oink · clomp · oink · oink · clomp

23

Water Play

Help the crocodile get to the pond by following the route with the time of the day in the correct order.

morning

night

afternoon

morning

evening

night

evening

Monthly matter

Follow the months of the year to find your way out of the maze.

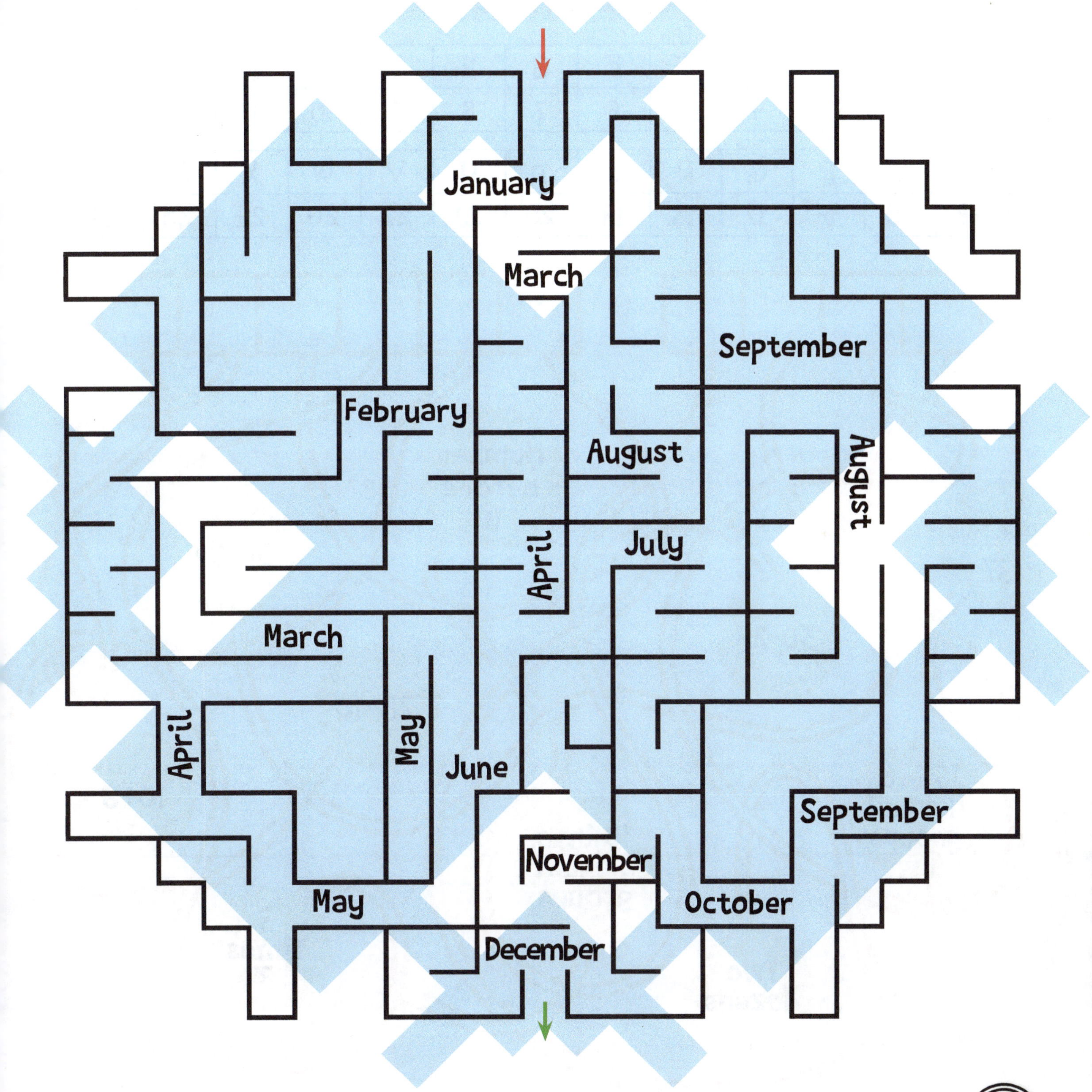

January

March

September

February

August

August

April

July

March

April

May

June

April

September

November

October

May

December

Hidden Message

Find the hidden word in the puzzle below. Solve the sums, then use the answers to find the code to fill in the letters.

A	B	C	D	E	F	G	H	I	J	K	L	M
1	2	3	4	5	6	7	8	9	10	11	12	13

N	O	P	Q	R	S	T	U	V	W	X	Y	Z
14	15	16	17	18	19	20	21	22	23	24	25	26

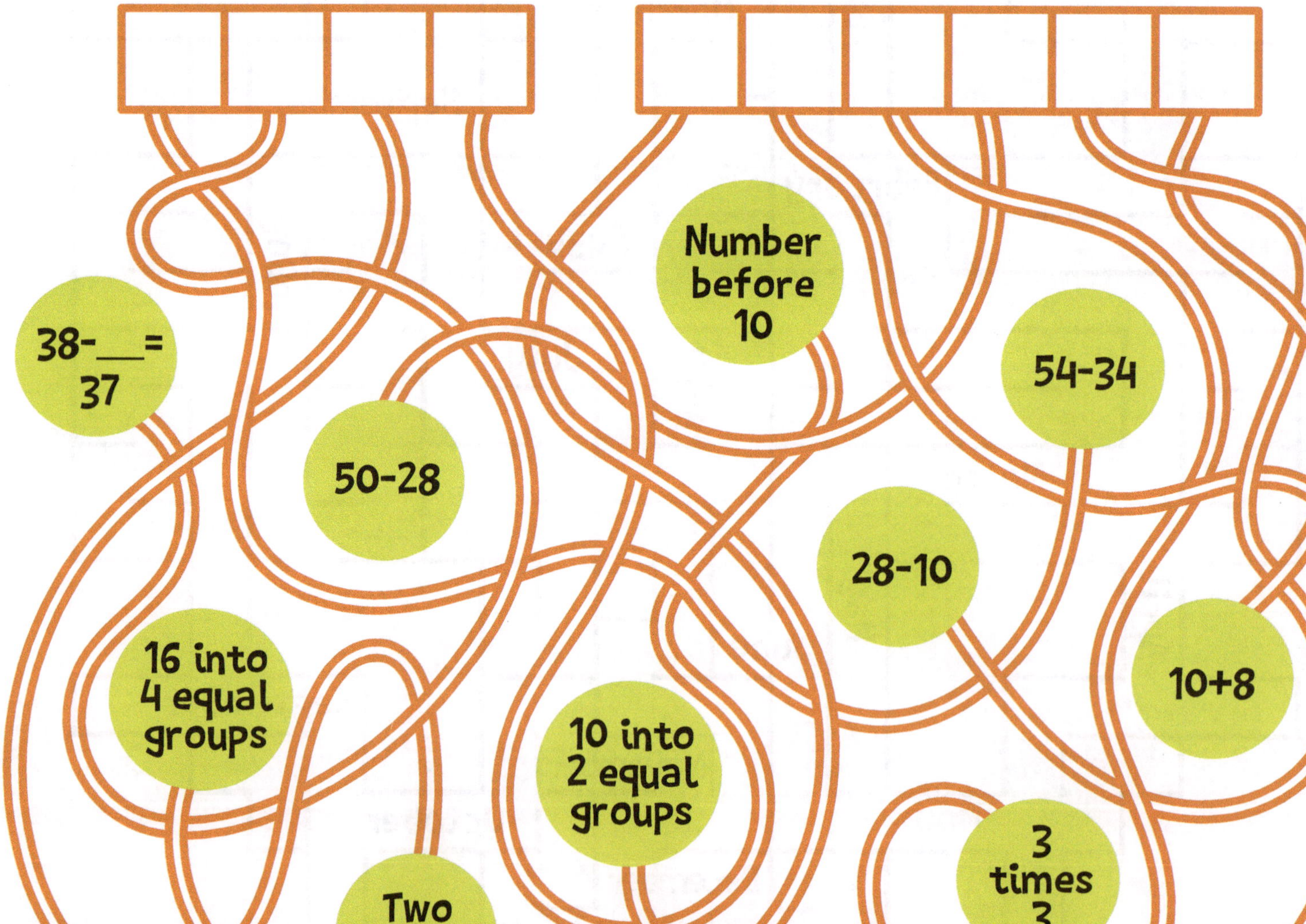

38-___= 37

50-28

Number before 10

54-34

28-10

16 into 4 equal groups

10 into 2 equal groups

10+8

Two dozens

3 times 3

99 - 82

Polygon Puzzle

Colour all the polygons in the maze below to find the path for Santa.

Math-It!

Polygons are closed figures with no curved lines.

Symmetrical Shapes

Follow the path to match one half of the shape to the other half. Remember to only match shapes that are symmetrical.

Math-It

Symmetrical shapes are those where both halves look like mirror images.

Shaped Up

Follow the path to match the 2D shapes with the similar 3D objects.

Math-it

3D shapes are called 3 dimensional shapes.

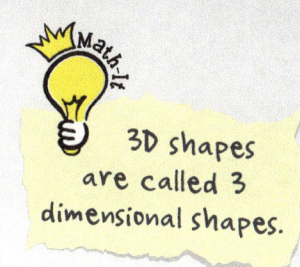

Math-o-Bot's Challenge

Help mother and baby have a fun day at the zoo. Take turns and roll the dice to know how many spaces each player moves.

There are 21 people in 3 big cars. How many people in one big car?

An insect has 6 legs. How many legs do 3 insects have?

There are 7 pens in one pack. How many pens in 2 packs?

There are 6 flowers in 3 vases. How many flowers in a vase?

16 frogs live in 4 ponds. How many frogs in each pond?

ZOO

Start

You must answer the questions to cross the block even if you do not land on it. Move one extra block every time you give a correct answer. Take 2 steps back for every incorrect answer.

One cat has 4 legs. How many legs to 5 cats have?

5 baskets have 15 apples. How many apples in each basket?

End

There are 3 wheels in a tricycle. How many wheels in 9 tricycles?

There are 6 juice cans in one box. How many juice cans in 5 boxes?

31

Dog and the Bone

Mark the quadrilaterals in the maze to help the dog get to the bone.

99 - 82

Hungry Kitty

If the cat's container is bigger than the cat food container, the cat will be able to get to it. Find the cats that will be able to reach the can. Remember that one cat can't take another cat's path.

56 - 31

Calculated Steps

Help the scientist get to his lab. He can only move in the 3 directions shown on the grid. He tried it once but fell short of it by four steps. Can you help him out?

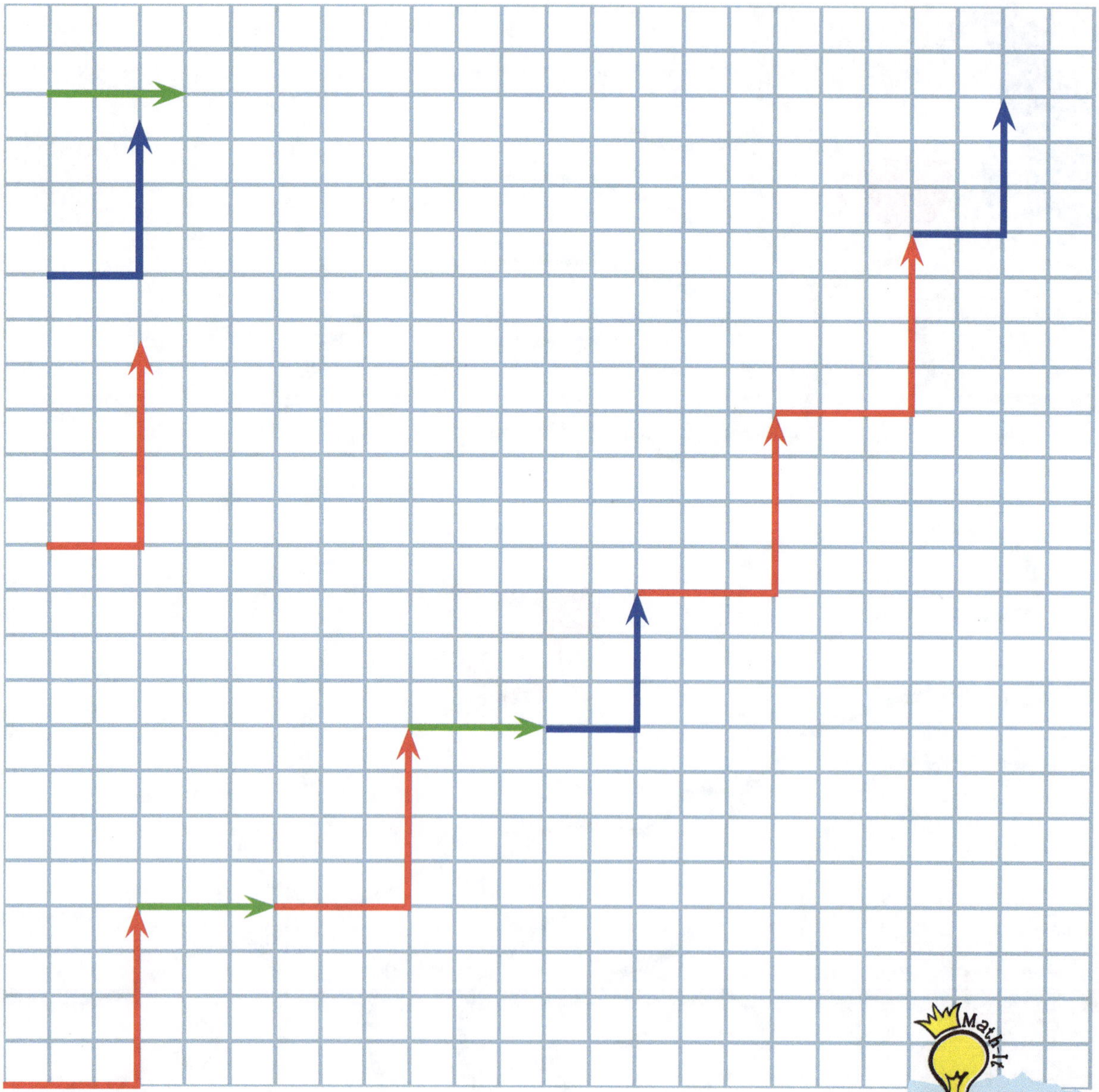

99 - 82

You may want to try going downwards.

Money Match

Follow the paths to see if the money shown on both sides is the same. The correct amount is the price for the chocolate.

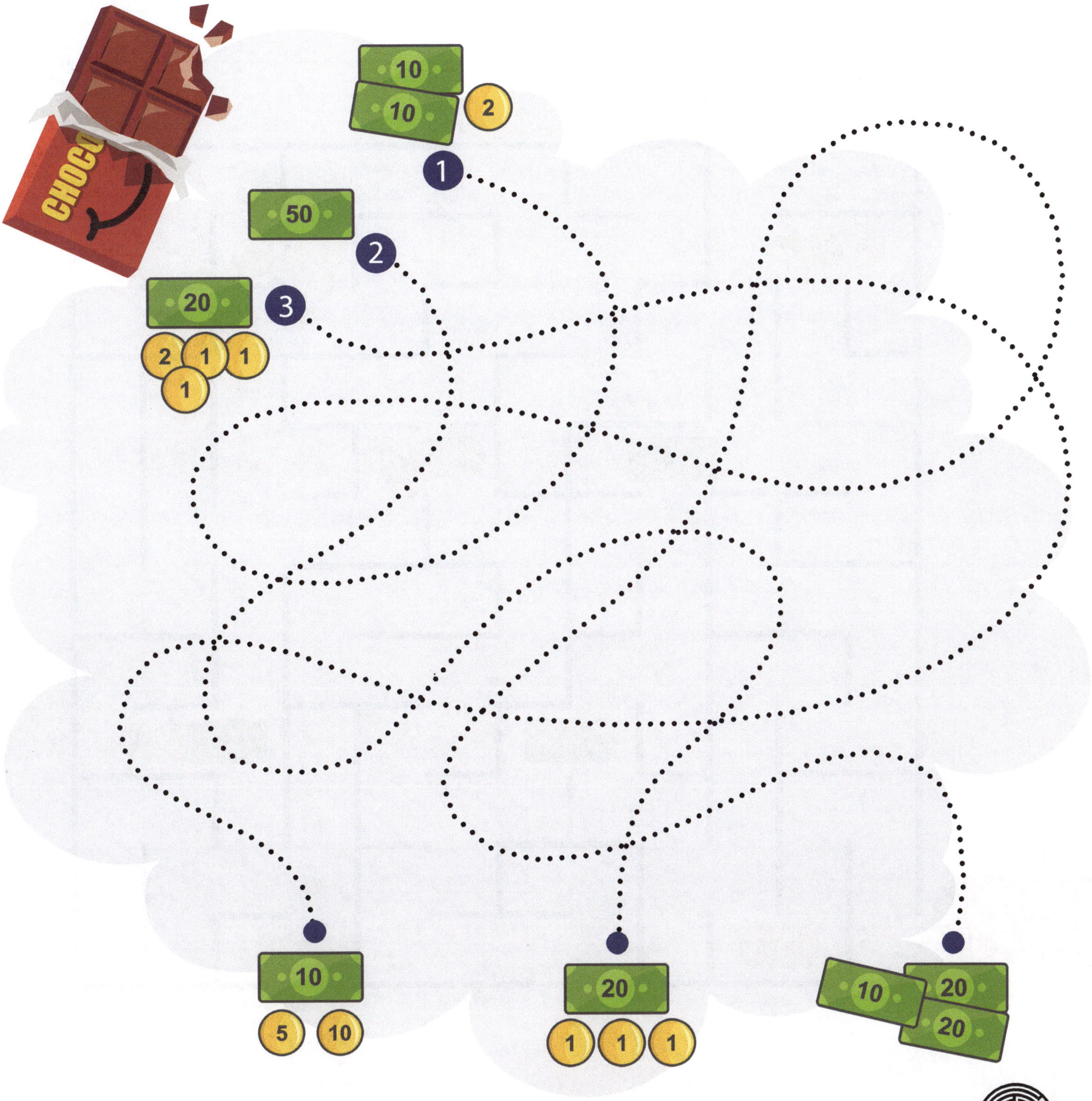

1 — 10, 10, 2

2 — 50

3 — 20, 2, 1, 1, 1

10, 5, 10

20, 1, 1, 1

10, 20, 20

Perfect Ten

Help the postman deliver the mail by following the path where the money equals ₹ 10.

Addition Subtraction

Find the way out of the maze by adding or subtracting the money mentioned. If the answer is less than ₹ 25, then you are on the right path.

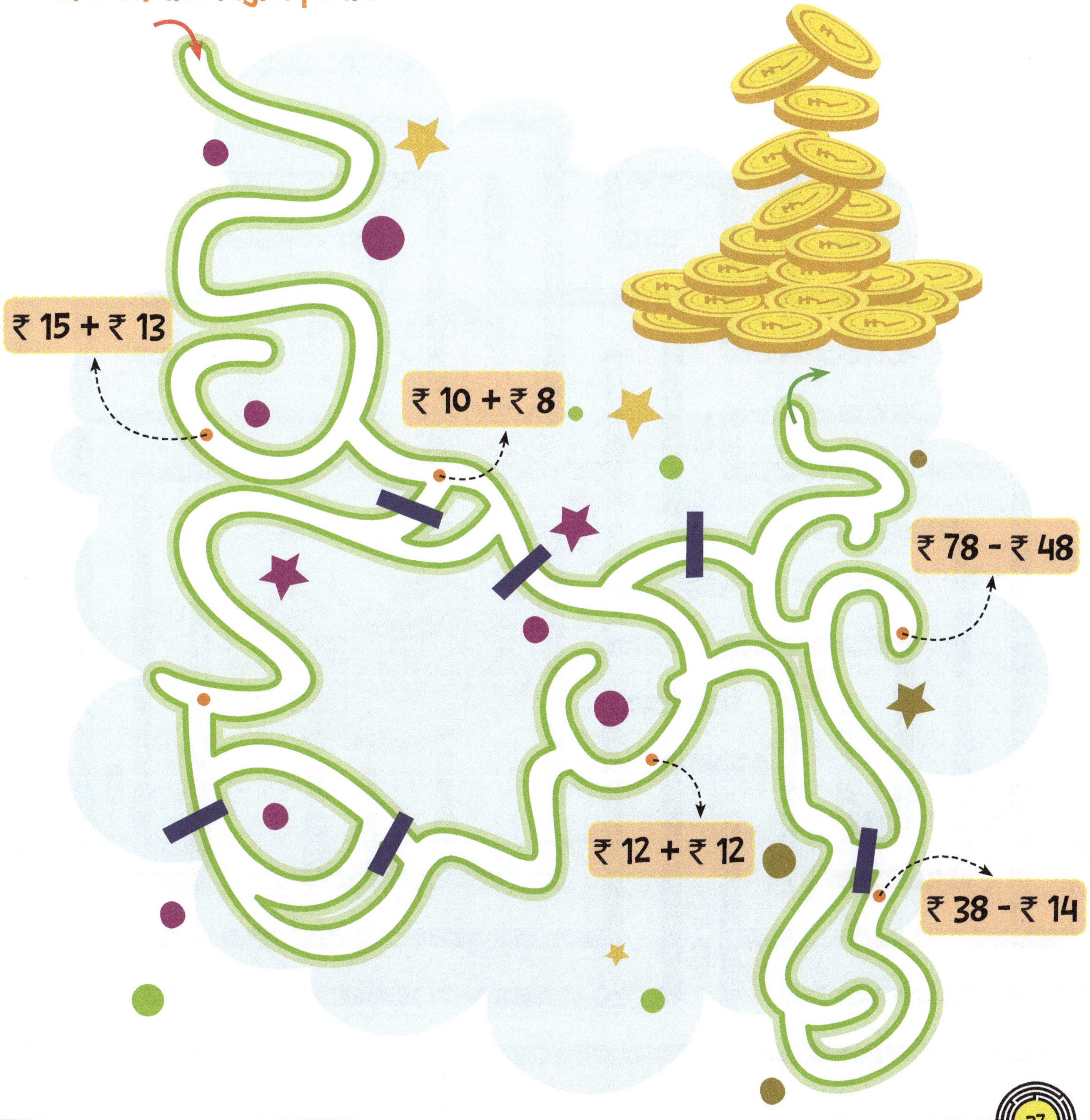

₹ 15 + ₹ 13

₹ 10 + ₹ 8

₹ 78 − ₹ 48

₹ 12 + ₹ 12

₹ 38 − ₹ 14

Save the Trees

Collect ₹ 100 on your way to save the trees.
Find a route to do so.

You may have to take a longer route.

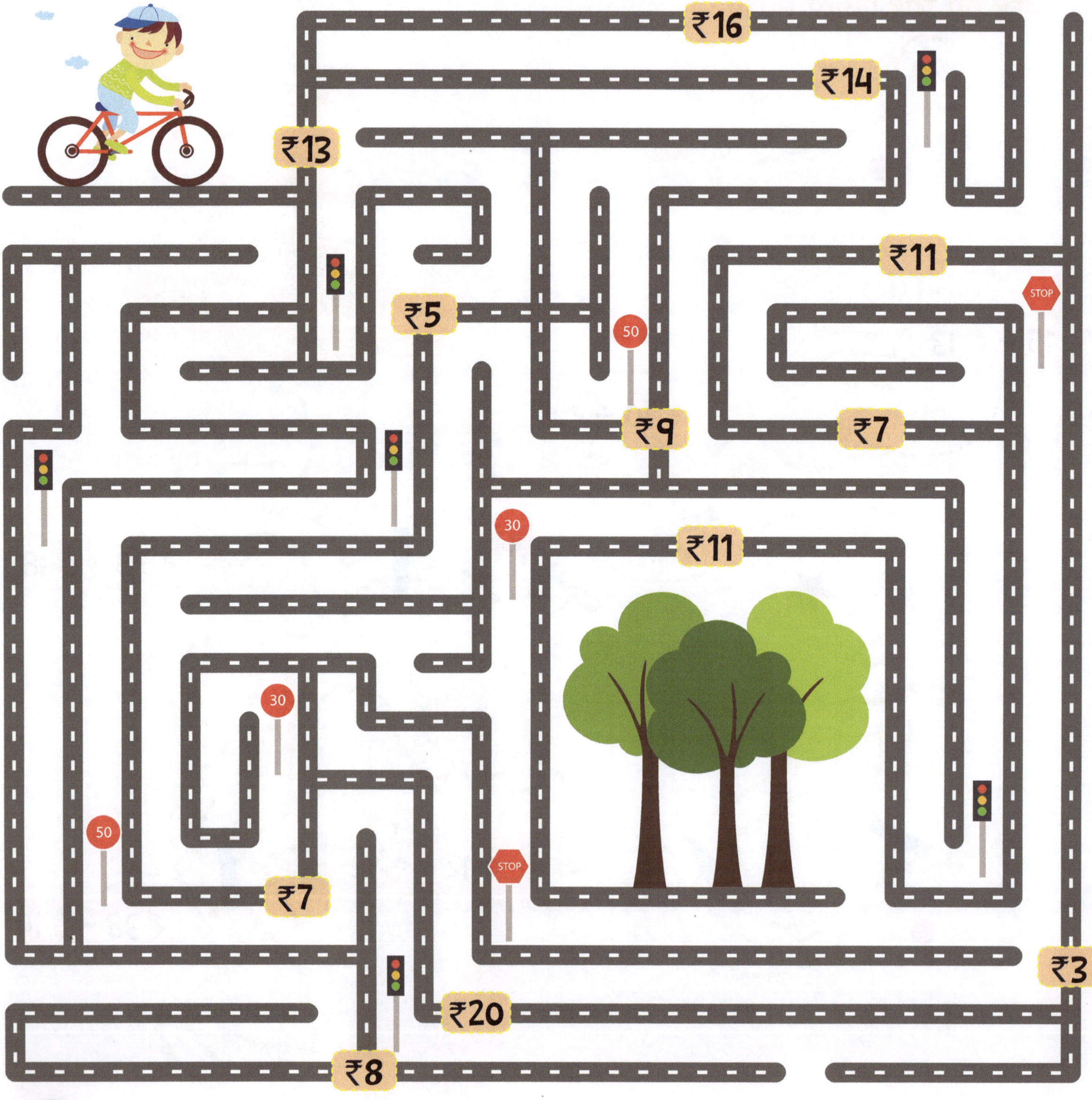

₹16 ₹14 ₹13 ₹11 ₹5 50 ₹9 ₹7 ₹11 30 ₹7 ₹3 ₹20 ₹8 50 30

Lost Giraffe

Help the lost baby giraffe reach its mother.
Follow the path by marking the time shown
on the clocks around the maze.

8 o'clock

6 o'clock

2 o'clock

5 o'clock

11 o'clock

10 o'clock

School Time

What time does school start? Trace the path from the clock to the school to find out when school starts.

99 - 82

Clockwork

Match the clocks and the timings mentioned. Find the shortest route possible.

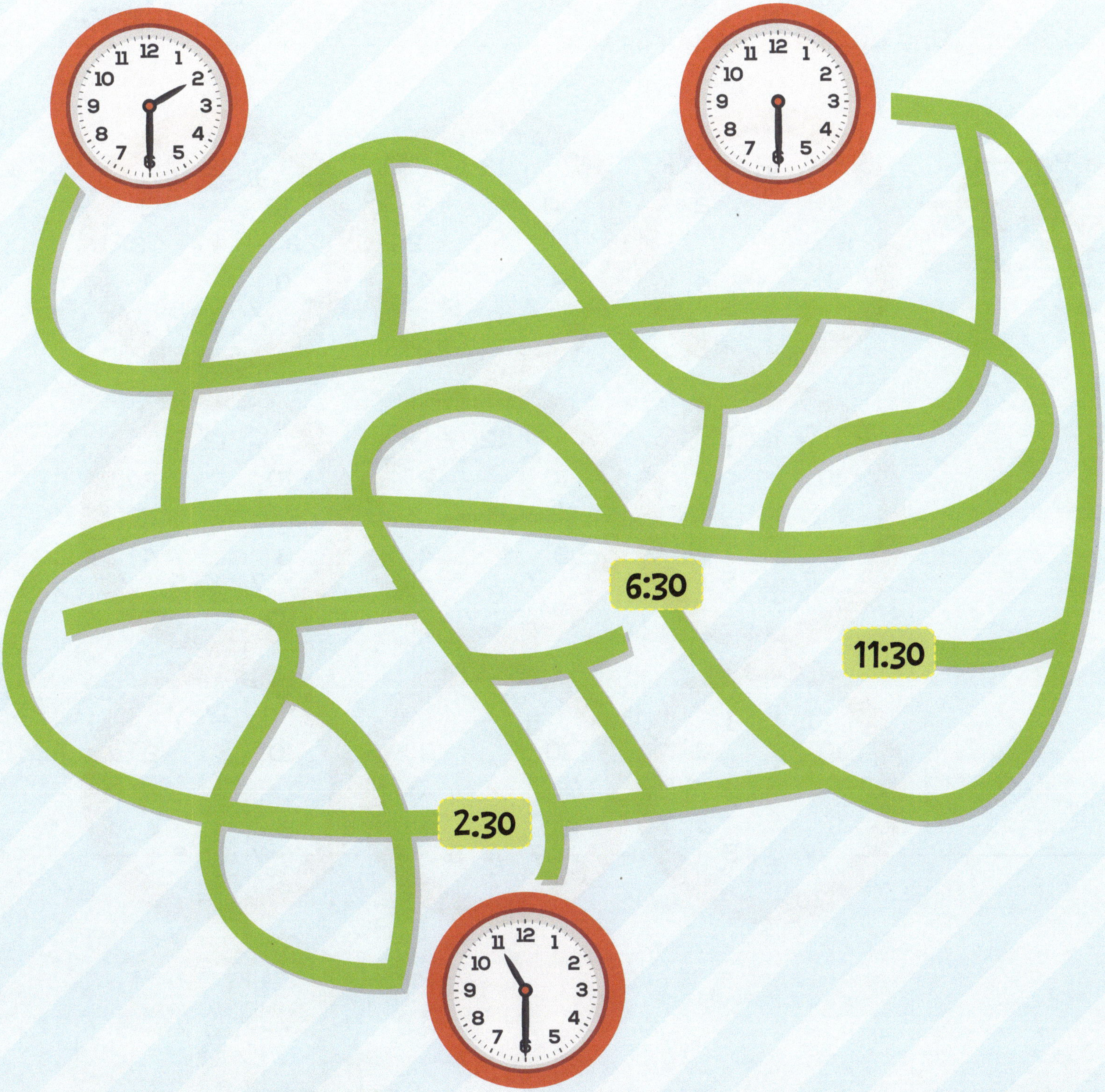

6:30

11:30

2:30

Time Travel

Draw the hands on the clock to create a path for the car to travel on. You may have to extend the hands to join them. Write the time alongside each clock. One has been done for you.

Math-ir
The time has to be to the closest 30 minutes.

Tweet Tweet

Match the tally marks with the numbers inside the maze, to help you find the right path between the birds.

Math-It: Five tallies are always put in a group.

6
3
4
10
7
9
11
15
12

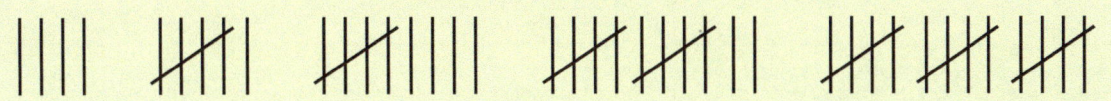

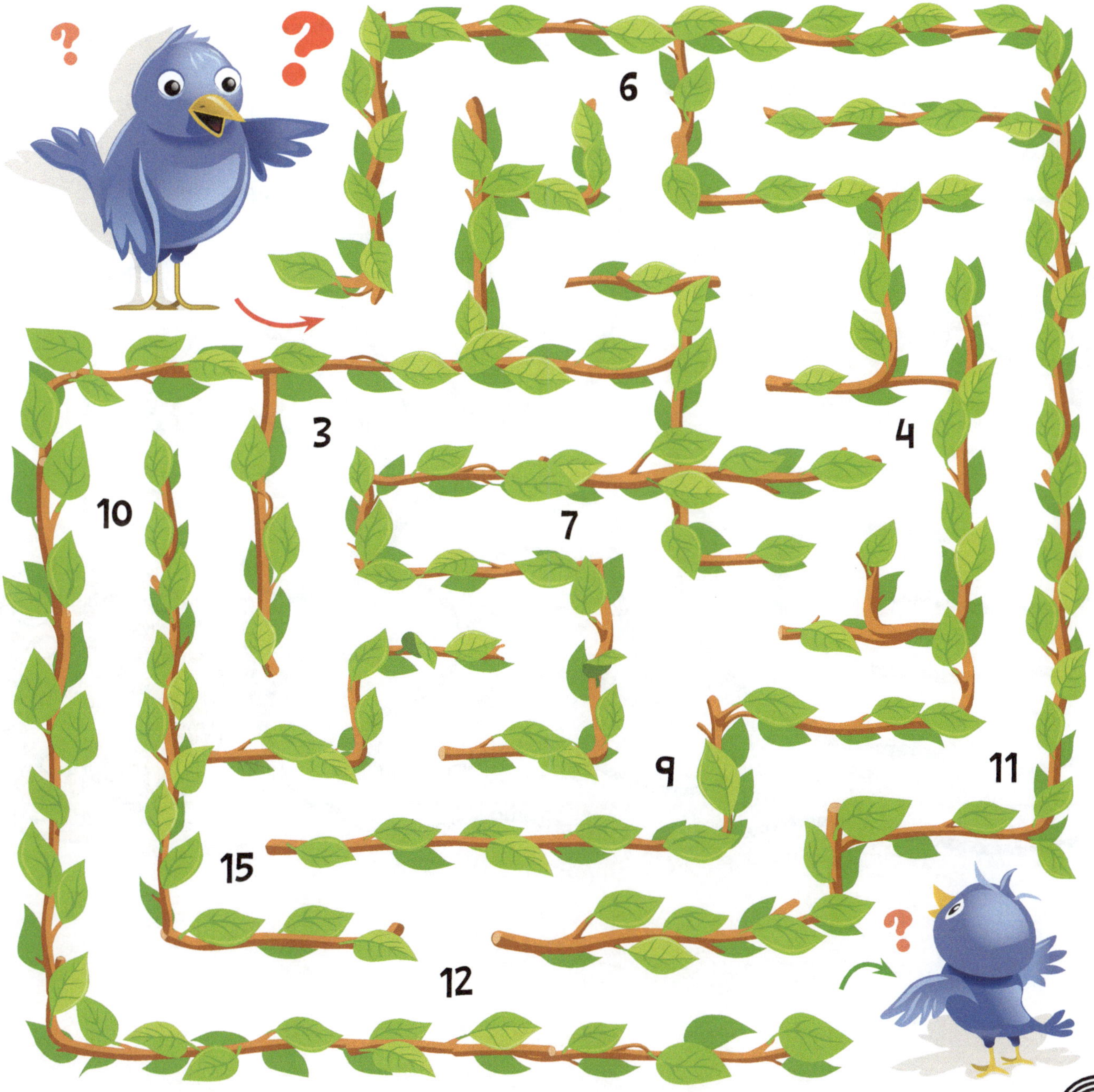

Pizza Time

Help the chef make yummy pizza. Take the route where the container can hold more pizza sauce to help find the correct path.

Answers

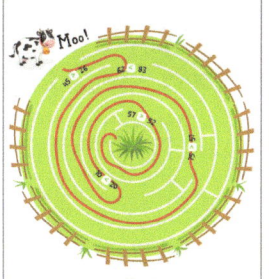

Page 3

Page 4

Page 5

Page 6

Page 7

Page 8

Page 9

Page 10

Page 11

Page 12

Page 13

Page 14

Page 15

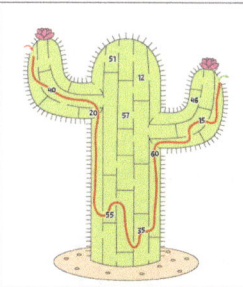

Page 16

Page 17

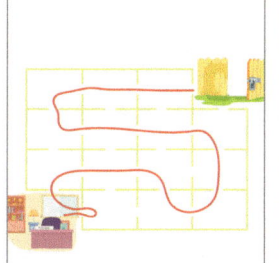

Page 18

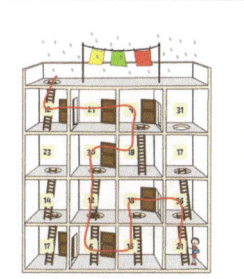

Page 19

Page 20

Page 21

Page 22

Page 23

Page 24

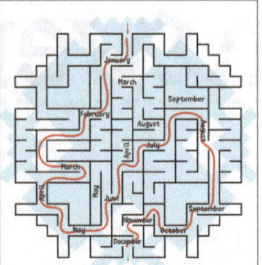

Page 25

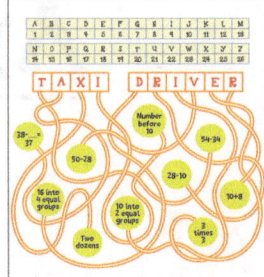

Page 26

Page 27

Page 28

Page 29

Page 30

Page 31

Page 32

Page 33

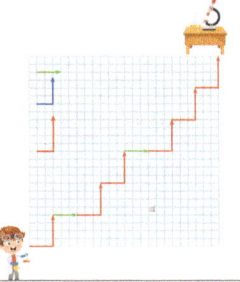

Page 34

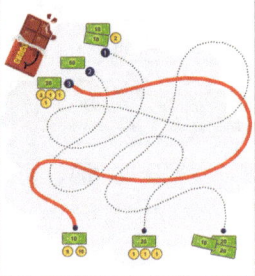

Page 35

Page 36

Page 37

Page 38

Page 39

Page 40

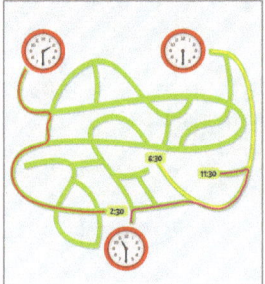

Page 41

Page 42

Page 43

Page 44